© **Ringpress Books**

An imprint of Interpet Publishing,
Interpet House, Vincent Lane,
Dorking, Surrey, RH4 3YX, UK

ISBN 13: 978-1-86054-259-6
ISBN 10: 1-86054-259-X

First published 2006. All rights reserved.
CARTOONS: Russell Jones.
DESIGN: Sarah Williams.
Printed and bound in China through SNP Leefung

CONTENTS

THE QUESTION OF GENDER
*The 'he' pronoun is used throughout this book in favour of
the rather impersonal 'it', but no gender bias is intended.*

INTRODUCTION

Cats make fantastic pets – they are loving, resourceful, entertaining and fantastic company for young and old alike. The good news doesn't stop there: they are also very easy to house train! If you've never had a pet before, or if you have only ever had dogs, you will be amazed at how simple the whole procedure can be with a cat. In many cases it's as simple as putting a litter tray in a room – the cat will find it and use it!

Of course, sometimes it's a little more difficult – which is where this book comes in – but even if you have a cat that persistently has accidents, soils a particular corner of the house, or who has an occasional mishap and you don't

HOUSE TRAINING

know why, then don't despair. Cats are pretty straightforward creatures, and it's usually easy to get to the bottom of why they behave as they do.

Firstly, it's important to understand a cat's natural behaviour. They are naturally clean creatures that have relied on good hygiene practices for their survival in the past. From early kittenhood their mothers would have encouraged them to toilet away from the nest, and to bury any urine and faeces. They do this to keep disease at bay and also to avoid alerting predators to the vulnerable kittens' whereabouts. Until the kittens were mobile, the mother would lick their bottoms to encourage them to toilet, and to clean them.

These instincts persist today. Cats hate to soil their 'dens', and are keen to find somewhere suitable to toilet. So, you are working with an eager, willing pupil. As long as you can meet his basic toileting requirements, he will happily oblige.

Sounds simple? It is!

COMMON SENSE

- Worm your cat regularly, following your vet's advice as to the preferred product and dosage.
- Pregnant women and those with suppressed immune systems should be particularly careful when changing cat litter, because of the small risk of Toxoplasmosis (which is also passed on through uncooked meat, etc.). Either get someone else to change the litter, or be especially careful not to come into contact with the contents.
- Faeces should be removed promptly.
- Wear plastic gloves when changing the litter and wash your hands thoroughly afterwards.

THE RIGHT MATERIALS

So, what are a cat's basic toileting requirements? Firstly, it's important to choose the most appropriate litter and litter tray. Some cats aren't fussy and will use whatever litter or tray you provide. Some are incredibly choosy, and will only use the finest-grain varieties, and show a marked preference for a particular type of tray. Most prefer the finer types but will use bulkier litter if that's all that's on offer (for example, if your usual type has sold out at the supermarket).

LITTER BUGS

To start off with, use the same litter that the cat is already familiar with – be it a clay-based, clumping, recycled paper/wood pellets, or fine-grain lightweight litter. The kitten's breeder, or the rescue shelter where he came from, can tell you what type to buy. The litter will then be easily recognisable to your new cat, and he should immediately recognise that it is to be used for toileting.

If the cat is reluctant to use the litter, then opt for a premium-quality small-grain type, which is the most comfortable to stand on and to dig.

If making a change to another type of litter, do so gradually. For example, if it is more convenient for you to buy a lightweight version, to avoid hernias or muscle strain, then put a little on the top of the cat's usual litter. Then, each time you change the tray, put more of the new litter in and less of the former litter, until a complete changeover has been achieved.

IN-TRAY

You can choose between a standard, open tray and a covered one. Some covered ones are all-singing, all-dancing, with filters in the lid for odour control, flaps at the front for access, and there are even self-cleaning varieties!

Some cats like the seclusion and safety of retiring to a covered tray; others don't like them at all. It's probably a good idea to start with a standard one, as they are so inexpensive, and to upgrade only if your cat needs to (for example, if he is being ambushed by other cats in the house, and likes the added security of a covered tray). Note: with asthmatic cats, covered trays should be avoided.

HOUSE TRAINING

THE RIGHT MATERIALS

Please don't buy a covered tray in the belief that, since it contains smells, you can get away with changing the litter less often. Cats hate to use dirty litter, and you will soon find accidents if you cut corners where cleaning and scooping are concerned. The tray should be cleaned regularly regardless of whether it's covered.

Whatever type of tray you choose, it should be deep enough for your cat to bury what he eliminates without overwhelming him. Usually pet shops or superstores sell a shallow tray for kittens and a deeper one for adults. Fill to between one-third to one-half of the depth, depending on your cat (some love burying and will appreciate having more litter; others just give a cursory tickle of the litter and can't wait to be gone from the tray).

Arthritic oldies would benefit from a shallow, uncovered tray that is easy for them to get in and out of. Don't overdo the litter, either – grey-whiskered moggies may feel unstable if they sink in mountains of the stuff.

There is an enormous range of litter trays available, but most cats will happily use a standard, open tray. Don't forget to buy a scoop as well, to remove your cat's deposits.

HOUSE TRAINING

OTHER BITS AND PIECES

In addition to the tray and litter, you should also purchase a slotted scoop, which lets litter – but not faeces – through, and also a non-slotted scoop for removing clumps of wet litter.

Use scented nappy sacks for the deposits. They can be tied securely and placed in the bin, which prevents any plumbing problems from flushing the litter down the loo.

Tray liners are also available, but are mostly unnecessary. They are easily torn when the cat scratches to bury his deposits. Some cats also end up 'gift wrapping' the entire tray, pulling the liner over the top so that, unless you get to the tray before he revisits, any subsequent deposits will slide off the top of the plastic instead of being absorbed in the litter.

Deodorisers are best avoided. If the litter smells, it should be cleaned. Masking the odour is no substitute for good husbandry, and such artificial pongs can irritate a cat's sensitive nose and may encourage him to find somewhere else to toilet instead.

A pet-safe disinfectant, available from pet stores, is necessary, to clean the tray thoroughly once a week.

LOCATION, LOCATION, LOCATION

Finding the right place for the litter tray is half the battle. You can have the best tray and the finest litter, but if it is in the wrong place, your cat will find his own toileting area. You'll quickly realise from the location of his 'accidents' that he prefers quiet, secluded places to relieve himself undisturbed.

Every home is different, so it's difficult to make a pronouncement as to where the litter tray should be positioned. One person's utility room may be a haven of tranquillity and entirely suitable for a litter tray, whereas another person's utility room may be a busy thoroughfare. Here are some guidelines:

- The tray should not be too close to the cat's food and drinking bowls. Would you like to eat lunch right next to your loo? Neither would your cat.
- The tray should be in a quiet location.
- Cats like corners. In the wild, a cat is vulnerable to predators when toileting. Having a litter tray in the middle of the room is not only impractical for you, it is also unnerving for cat, as he will feel exposed to possible attacks from all sides. So opt for a secluded spot, where your cat will feel safe. This is particularly important for nervous moggies and in multi-cat households where a toileting cat may be considered 'fair game' by a mischievous mog intent on ambushes.
- Also consider any other potential threats to a cat's security. Some nervous felines get spooked by seeing a

HOUSE TRAINING

neighbourhood cat passing by the other side of a cat-flap or peeping in through a window, or even by post coming in through the letterbox.

• You can't have too many litter trays. One upstairs and one downstairs is a good starting point with a kitten, and also with an older mog, that may be a little arthritic. Three litter trays, distributed around the house, is recommended for two cats; four trays for three cats, and so on.

GETTING STARTED

In 99.9 per cent of cases, if you have the right trays, the right litter, and the right location, your cat will work out the rest for himself. But sometimes, it is necessary to lend a helping paw.

- With a clean tray and fresh litter, put the kitten in the tray, and then dig with your hand. There's little point in holding your cat's paw and encouraging him to dig – it will probably spook him, and you want him to build up positive associations with the tray.
- You could also try putting him in the tray after he's eaten, after he wakes, and after a period of play. He is more likely to want to toilet at these times, so you may pre-empt any accidents.
- If you spot any warning signs that a loo visit is necessary (see page 14), you could also put him in the tray.

Normally, it is not necessary for the owner to intervene – most cats work it out for themselves.

With a young kitten, you can speed up house training by placing him in the tray after he has eaten.

- If your moggie is nervous, however, it may not be wise to interfere. If too much attention stresses him, then you will do more harm than good by putting him in the tray repeatedly. Instead, leave him to it. If the tray meets all his needs, he should use it.

With new cats, it is recommended that they be kept in a small, quiet room at first, while they are settling in. This room should contain a litter tray. With few distractions, and with the tray easily within reach, it would be unusual for a kitten not to use it.

If he does have an accident, and hasn't realised what the tray is for, you could collect a small amount of his urine and put it in his tray (use disposable gloves, and an absorbent sponge to mop up the mess before squeezing out the urine in the tray or dabbing it on the top of the litter, depending on how much of a puddle there has been). Don't go overboard, though – if he considers the tray to be dirty, he will be reluctant to use it. Do be sure to clean up the site of the accident thoroughly, so he doesn't return to toilet there again (see page 23).

It is rare for intervention to be necessary – even with feral kittens who may have been separated from mum at an early age. Toileting really is instinctive.

SPOTTING THE SIGNS

Cats rarely eliminate without giving prior warning. Your cat may be restless, looking around the house for a suitable place to relieve himself, or, particularly if he's adult, he may loiter around the back door, hoping to be let outside. He may be vocal, literally asking if he can be excused! He will probably go to a quiet corner somewhere, before scratching the ground, circling to position himself, and then squatting.

- If you see any of these signs, immediately pick him up and take him to his tray.
- Do not react angrily, just be calm and act quickly.
- Once you've put him in the tray, step away, look away and be unassuming. Hovering over him could unnerve him; even talking to him could distract his attention.
- If he finishes his business in the tray, let him bury it and leave the tray in his own time. Then reward him with lots of cat sweet-talk – tell him what a wonderful boy he is, and stroke and love him.
- If you didn't quite get to him in time, put any accident in the tray, before cleaning the area thoroughly (page 23).

Never rub your cat's nose in the mess. This is cruelty beyond description. It does not teach a cat anything other than the fact that you are a person who should be avoided at all costs. A cat will not understand why you are punishing him; he will not make the association that he has used the wrong place. If anything, such action could actually encourage him to be more furtive in the future. He may believe that you are displeased simply because he has toileted (rather than *where* he has toileted) and so may hide away from you to relieve himself.

See also When Accidents Happen, page 20.

HOUSE TRAINING

THE GREAT OUTDOORS

Unless your cat is a permanent house-cat, either through necessity or through your choice, the time will come when you will want to introduce him to the great outdoors.

However, you should not dispense with the indoor litter tray. For safety's sake, all cats should be kept indoors when it is dark. Cats are crepuscular, meaning they are most active at dawn and dusk, when they hunt their prey. At these times, they are oblivious to other dangers – when in pursuit of a mouse, they are unlikely to stop at the kerbside to ensure it is safe to cross! And, of course, when it is dark, cats are less visible to drivers. Because most feline road deaths happen at night, the cat should be called in just before darkness falls, and the cat-flap should be locked until morning. Expecting your cat to keep his legs crossed all night is asking too much, so the indoor litter tray should remain available.

Some cats even prefer to use their indoor litter tray during the day – not only in bad weather, when they don't want to get their paws wet – but also on the sunniest of days. Some cats just like to toilet at home, and will often

come in from lazing around in the garden, to use their tray, before returning outside again. This is great for gardeners, and for those with green-fingered neighbours.

It's also useful to keep an eye on your cat's toileting habits. For example, if he is urinating a lot more, or there's a change in the consistency of his faeces, you should seek veterinary advice. Also consult your vet if you notice he has difficulty passing urine or faeces, if there's blood in the tray, if worms are present, or if you notice anything else that is unusual. All these factors cannot be assessed if your cat toilets outside and buries the evidence.

HOUSE TRAINING

THE GREAT OUTDOORS

Introducing outdoor toileting is often just a case of letting mog outside, and he'll find his own spot. But some cats need a little more guidance. It is also useful to train him to use a particular area of your garden, so that you can protect your flower beds.

• First, prepare a place in your garden that you don't mind sacrificing as a feline outdoor loo. Remember that cats do not like to feel exposed when toileting, so a quiet corner will be more successful than an open spot.

Cats allowed access to the great outdoors will quickly choose a preferred spot to relieve themselves.

- Dig an area at least one metre square, and hoe it, so that there are no large lumps of earth. Remove all stones, so that the earth is soft and comfortable for puss to dig with his paws.
- Take a little used litter marked with your cat's urine from your cat's tray, and scatter it over the top of the freshly dug area.
- Some trainers advocate slowly moving kitty's litter tray closer to the back door, over a period of a week or so, and then moving it outside the door, and then finally into the garden. However, this approach may not be very successful if, as recommended, you continue to keep a litter tray for inside use. If you just encourage puss to the area you have prepared in the garden, he should use it – provided the ground is comfortable for him to paw, and the location is secluded.
- Once a week, dig the soil over, to keep it fresh.
- Keep children away from the area, and keep any sandpits covered when not in use, in case mog decides to use those instead.

NOT THERE!

If your cat decides on his own spot in the garden, and it is acceptable to you, then great. If it is not convenient, then assess why he prefers this area to the one you have prepared for him.

Having made the necessary adjustments (moved location to an area that is more sheltered, perhaps), you need to dissuade him from using the other area. This can be done by putting gravel, crushed egg shells, or medium-sized pebbles on the surface. This kind of substrate is difficult to dig, and will not be comfortable for mog to walk on.

WHEN ACCIDENTS HAPPEN

Accidents are rare. Most kittens or adult cats, whatever their background, walk into your home, suss out where the tray is, and use it. End of story. It's all so simple! But, during a cat's lifetime, there may be the occasional accident, or, for whatever reason, he may suddenly refuse to use his tray.

ASSESS THE MESS

Cats behave as they do for a reason, so it is necessary to do some detective work to find out why he's having accidents.

• How clean is the tray? Even if you've been scooping regularly, it still needs at least one complete change of litter and a good clean once a week.

Accidents in the house are rare. If your cat's house training lapses, you need to work out why.

- Are there sufficient trays for the number of cats you have? See page 11.
- Do you know the culprit? In a multi-cat household, be absolutely sure that you know the identity of the erring cat, so that you can accurately assess why he is behaving as he is. And if veterinary advice needs to be sought, there's no point taking Tigger to the clinic for a check-up if Tibbles is actually the one responsible for the puddles!
- Check the site of the tray. Even if your cat has happily used the tray there for a number of years, perhaps something has now spooked him. For example, perhaps a firework bang and flash or thunder and lightning scared him when he used it, and now he wants somewhere away from a window, or just in a new location that doesn't have bad memories for him. See page 10.
- Think about your home circumstances. Has anything changed that could have upset him? A new lodger, a change in routine, or even just the owners being stressed about something can affect a sensitive cat. If he feels anxious, then he may want even more security when toileting, so will seek a small, dark, safe corner somewhere. If you think stress is the cause, then remedy whatever is causing it. In addition, buy some Feliway from your vet. This product, in the form of a spray or diffuser, replicates the calming properties of cat facial pheromones. Cats rub against furniture or doors and other items, to surround themselves in the smell and to help them feel happy and secure. Using Feliway should produce the same results and reduce or eliminate your cat's anxiety.
- Have you changed the type of cat litter, and he is voicing his distaste? Or have you used a deodoriser? See pages 6-9.

HOUSE TRAINING

- Most cats revisit the site of previous accidents, so bar him access to this area for a few days. This should help to break the habit, and will encourage him to find somewhere else. The litter tray should meet all his needs; if it doesn't, assess why he doesn't want to use it.
- If he keeps returning to the same spot, perhaps the smell is attracting him. See Clean-Up Operation.
- Are you sure he is urinating and not scent-marking? See page 24.

CLEAN-UP OPERATION

Don't make the mistake of thinking that an area is clean just because it smells clean to you – cats have really sensitive noses and can detect the odour of previous accidents very easily.

Similarly, the majority of popular household cleaners actually attract cats to them! This is because ammonia and chlorine – found in most products – are also present in cat urine! So, either use a product made specifically for cleaning accidents (ask your pet store or vet for details) or follow the regime below…

- Use a solution of biological washing powder, diluted in warm water, to clean any accident site. This will remove the protein from the urine stain.
- Now rinse the area thoroughly, and, when it is dry, dab the site with surgical spirit and again allow to dry.
- Please note: whatever product you use, exercise caution, testing a small, hidden part of any material first to ensure that it will not be damaged. Remember also to keep your cat away from the area.

- If the accidents persist, or you cannot understand why they have started, you should seek veterinary advice. Sometimes there is a physical cause for a lapse in house training, such as cystitis.

HOUSE TRAINING

There may be a medical reason for your cat's failure to use the litter tray, so seek veterinary advice if accidents persist.

SCENT-MARKING

It is important not to confuse a lapse in house training with scent-marking. When a cat urinates, he squats and releases a fair amount of liquid on to the ground. When a cat scent-marks, he usually stands on all fours, and squirts out a short jet of liquid on to a vertical surface, such as a tree or the side of the sofa. However, he can also squat and scent-mark, and he may even leave faeces in prominent places, too (which is called 'middening').

It is not unusual for duvets, laundry, or anything else that smells of the owner, to be marked by the cat, in his attempt to mingle his scent in with that of his 'protector'.

FELINE STRESS

Remember: it's not just the presence of hostile neighbourhood cats that can cause kitty stress. Perhaps another of your cats is intimidating him? Make sure he has a room of his own that he can retreat to – such as your bedroom – away from other felines.

Male and female cats can scent-mark, regardless of whether they have been neutered. However, most offenders are entire toms (unneutered male cats), which tend to be more territorial than their female or neutered counterparts. This is the key to scent-marking– it is a cat's way of marking out an area. It acts as an olfactory fence to other cats, warning them that they are trespassing, and it also reassures the scent-marker, who is surrounded by his familiar scent.

These smelly messages to other cats reveal all sorts of things about the sprayer – gender, age, reproductive ability, and so on – but the messages have to be reinforced, as they fade. This is why it is so difficult to stop a cat from scent-marking – as he has to top up the scent regularly.

Certainly, neutering is worth discussing with your vet, as it should reduce a cat's territorial nature. If the sprayer is already neutered then stress is the most likely cause of the behaviour, with mog anxiously trying to keep other cats away and reassuring himself with his own scent-marking.

Removing the cause of his stress and using Feliway spray or diffuser (see page 23) should be your first step. If the spraying continues, talk to your vet, who can refer you to a reputable feline behaviourist. Untreated, spraying not only causes the owner great tension, but clearly shows that mog is anxious, too. Getting to the root of the problem quickly should make it easier to solve, and should prevent any health problems that are associated with long-term stress.

PROBLEM-SOLVING

OAP: OLD AGE CAT

BACKGROUND

Twelve-year-old Stella had been with the Martin family since she was a kitten. She had always been the perfect pet (apart from a wild, curtain-climbing period in her youth!), and had never had an accident in the house. Then, the Martins began to notice piles and puddles just next to Stella's litter tray – and then, a few months later, upstairs in the box-room.

CAUSE

Initially, the Martins believed that Stella was perching too far back in the litter tray and so was toileting on the floor by accident. They bought a covered tray, to stop this happening, but still they continued to find the accidents next to the tray.

They set up a camcorder to film the litter tray, and, playing it back, saw what the problem was – Stella found it difficult to get into the tray. She attempted getting in, but then gave up and relieved herself as close to the tray as she could, but on the floor.

The Martins had noticed that Stella had become less mobile than she once was, but had failed to realise the toileting implications.

If she was upstairs asleep, even the trek down the stairs to the litter tray became too much of an effort, and so she took to using the little-used box-room, too.

TREATMENT

The covered tray, and the former deep tray, were replaced with a shallow one (used by kittens). Less litter was put in the tray – enough for Stella to bury her business, but not enough to make her unsteady when she stepped into the tray. Another tray was placed in the box-room, so that Stella had easy access to the loo wherever she was in the house.

A trip to the vet was also organised, for a mobility supplement and pain relief. Until the accidents, the Martins simply hadn't realised how debilitating Stella's arthritis was – they had just put it down to the usual slowing down that happens with old age.

Within eight weeks, there was some improvement in Stella's mobility, though the Martins continued to use the two shallow trays, up and down stairs. To date, the home has been accident-free.

TEACH YOUR CAT

PRIVACY PROBLEMS

BACKGROUND

Bentley, a year-old house-cat, could be a little nervous and skittish at times. When strangers came to the house, he would hide, but would return to his usual self once they left. Loud noises also spooked him, but, generally, he was a happy boy who enjoyed life.

He had experienced a few house training problems when he was a kitten, as he was being bullied by a neighbour's cat. During this time he refused to use the litter tray by the backdoor, where he could see the outside yard and any passing cats. For almost nine months, though, since the tray was moved to the front hall, Bentley had been entirely clean in the house. But then accidents started to appear…

CAUSE

It was no coincidence that the accidents started soon after his owners, John and Carole Hadley, introduced Bella, a rescued dog, to the home. They were surprised at the toileting lapse, though, as Bentley and Bella got on amazingly well. An older dog, used to living with a cat, Bella was very respectful of her feline house-mate, and, after an initial few days of hiding, Bentley quickly realised that Bella was no threat and so got on with life as usual.

The Hadleys still thought that stress was responsible for the toileting lapses, though, and so used a hormone diffuser close to Bentley's bed – but the accidents continued, and so they called in an animal behaviourist.

It seemed that stress was the cause – but only when Bentley was actually attempting to toilet. When Bella was shut away from the hall (where the litter tray was located), Bentley quickly returned to using it. As soon as the door was opened, however, Bella made a dive for the tray and ate the faeces!

It appeared that her eagerness for such doggie delicacies didn't stop if Bentley was actually in the middle of using the tray – and this, understandably, upset him!

TREATMENT

Bentley's litter tray was moved upstairs, and a child-gate was put across the bottom of the stairs. This prevented Bella access to the tray and its contents, but allowed athletic Bentley to leap over the gate to toilet undisturbed when the need arose.

Problem sorted!

FAIR-WEATHER FELINE

BACKGROUND

Fifi, a seven-month-old Persian, loved her creature comforts. Like any self-respecting cat, she longed for laps and thrived on adoration!

She took to house training easily as a kitten, but when she was allowed outside, her owner, Jane Marsh, removed the indoor tray altogether. Fifi took to toileting outside with no problems, but, after a few weeks, she had an accident in the house – by the back door. A few days later, the same thing happened once more – again, by the cat-flap. Sometimes she would be clean for weeks, and then, seemingly for no good reason, she would toilet inside again.

CAUSE

Jane wracked her brains as to why Fifi was behaving as she was, and finally contacted her local cat charity for advice. She was advised to keep a diary, in which to record anything significant that happened in the day – not just Fifi's toilet habits (the time and nature of the accidents), but also whether visitors came, whether there were fireworks, what the weather conditions were, what Fifi was fed, her general mood, and so on.

Six weeks later, a charity volunteer went through the diary with Jane, and they quickly noticed a pattern. On the days when Fifi toileted indoors, it had rained! In a nutshell, Fifi didn't like getting wet!

TREATMENT

The solution was simple – an indoor litter tray. The charity volunteer advised that Fifi should be kept indoors anyway after dark, so a litter tray would be necessary for night-times as well as for rainy days.

The tray was placed near the back door, where Fifi had shown a preference for toileting, and she used it in wet weather and whenever she was shut inside after dark.

OVER TO YOU...

Cats are the most wonderful pupils when it comes to house training. In fact, the vast majority are self-taught, and are fully conversant with a litter tray – and what they need to do in it – before they ever set foot in your home.

If there are problems, though, they are usually easily solved – provided you treat your cat kindly, consider the world from his eyes, and are not afraid of seeking professional help if progress is limited.

Good luck!